Teaching Little Fingers to Play
More Broadway Songs

10 Piano Solos with Optional Teacher Accompaniments
Arranged by
Carolyn Miller

CONTENTS

Book
ISBN 978-1-4584-1767-1

Book/CD
ISBN 978-1-4584-1768-8

WILLIS MUSIC

EXCLUSIVELY DISTRIBUTED BY

HAL•LEONARD®
CORPORATION
7777 W. BLUEMOUND RD. P.O. BOX 13819 MILWAUKEE, WI 53213

Visit Hal Leonard Online at
www.halleonard.com

Oh, What a Beautiful Mornin'

from OKLAHOMA!

Optional Teacher Accompaniment

Lyrics by Oscar Hammerstein II
Music by Richard Rodgers
Arranged by Carolyn Miller

Like a waltz, in 1

Oh, What a Beautiful Mornin'
from OKLAHOMA!

TRACK 1-2

Play both hands one octave higher when performing as a duet.

Lyrics by Oscar Hammerstein II
Music by Richard Rodgers
Arranged by Carolyn Miller

Memory
from CATS

Optional Teacher Accompaniment

Music by Andrew Lloyd Webber
Text by Trevor Nunn after T.S. Eliot
Arranged by Carolyn Miller

Moderato, flowing

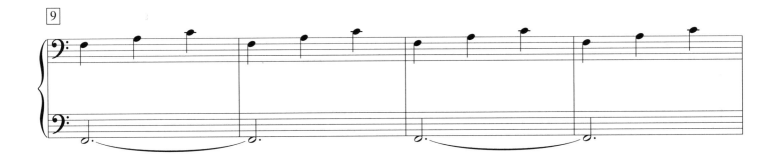

Memory
from CATS

Music by Andrew Lloyd Webber
Text by Trevor Nunn after T.S. Eliot
Arranged by Carolyn Miller

 TRACK 3-4

Play both hands one octave higher when performing as a duet.

Moderato, flowing

Accompaniment

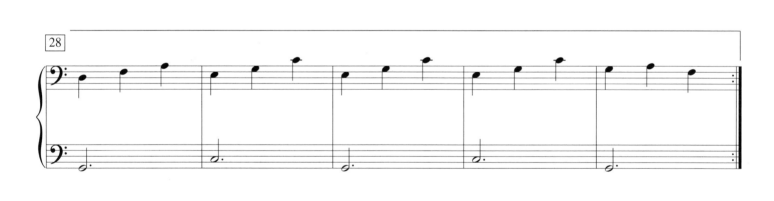

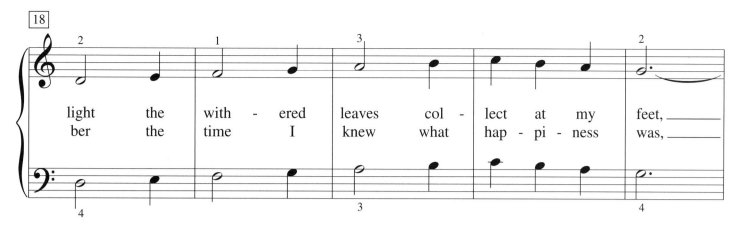

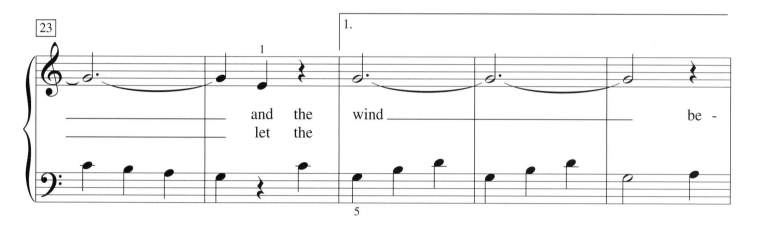

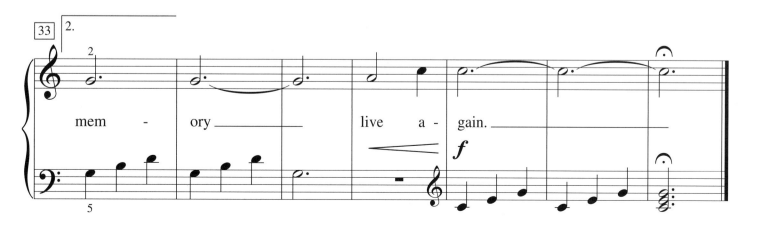

Think of Me
from THE PHANTOM OF THE OPERA

Optional Teacher Accompaniment

Music by Andrew Lloyd Webber
Lyrics by Charles Hart
Additional Lyrics by Richard Stilgoe
Arranged by Carolyn Miller

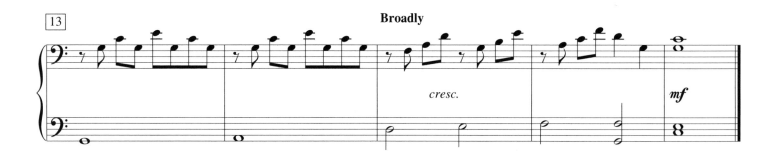

Think of Me

from THE PHANTOM OF THE OPERA

Music by Andrew Lloyd Webber
Lyrics by Charles Hart
Additional Lyrics by Richard Stilgoe
Arranged by Carolyn Miller

TRACK 5-6

Play both hands one octave higher when performing as a duet.

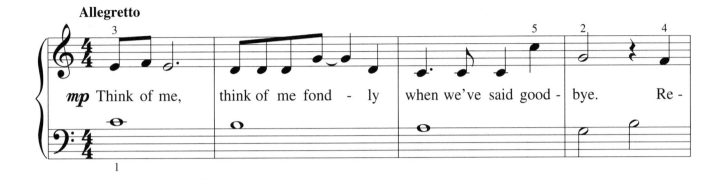

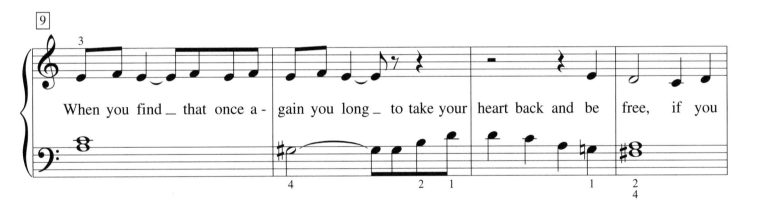

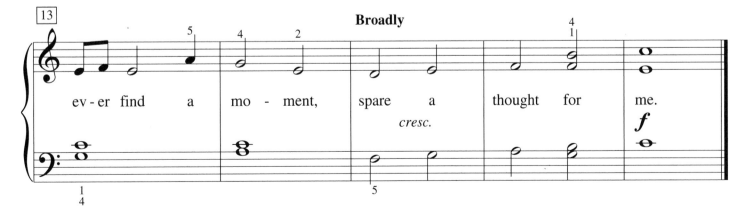

Castle on a Cloud
from LES MISÉRABLES

Optional Teacher Accompaniment

Note to teacher:
This arrangement presents an opportune time to reinforce the meaning of "time signature."
3 = three beats per measure
2 = half note gets the beat

Music by Claude-Michel Schönberg
Lyrics by Alain Boublil, Jean-Marc Natel
and Herbert Kretzmer
Arranged by Carolyn Miller

Longingly, not too slow

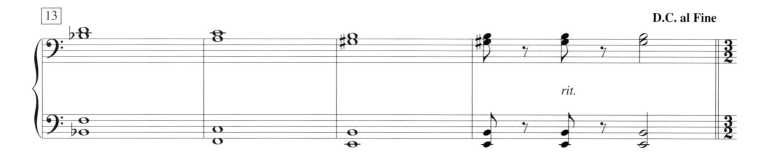

Castle on a Cloud
from LES MISÉRABLES

Music by Claude-Michel Schönberg
Lyrics by Alain Boublil, Jean-Marc Natel
and Herbert Kretzmer
Arranged by Carolyn Miller

TRACK 7-8

Play both hands one octave higher when performing as a duet.

Longingly, not too slow

There is a cas-tle on a cloud. I like to go there in my sleep.
I know a place where no one's lost. I know a place where no one cries.

Aren't an-y floors for me to sweep,
Cry-ing at all is not al-lowed,
not in my cas-tle on a cloud.

There is a la-dy all in white, holds me and sings a lull-a-by. She's

nice to see, and she's soft to touch. She says, "Co-sette, I love you ver-y much."

Where Is Love?
from the Broadway Musical OLIVER!

Optional Teacher Accompaniment

Words and Music by
Lionel Bart
Arranged by Carolyn Miller

Where Is Love?

from the Broadway Musical OLIVER!

Words and Music by
Lionel Bart
Arranged by Carolyn Miller

TRACK
9-10

Play both hands one octave higher when performing as a duet.

It's the Hard-Knock Life

from the Musical Production ANNIE

Optional Teacher Accompaniment

Lyric by Martin Charnin
Music by Charles Strouse
Arranged by Carolyn Miller

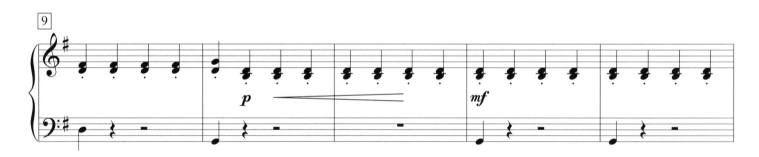

It's the Hard-Knock Life
from the Musical Production ANNIE

TRACK 11-12

Play both hands one octave higher when performing as a duet.

Lyric by Martin Charnin
Music by Charles Strouse
Arranged by Carolyn Miller

In My Own Little Corner
from CINDERELLA

Optional Teacher Accompaniment

Lyrics by Oscar Hammerstein II
Music by Richard Rodgers
Arranged by Carolyn Miller

Dreamily, not too slow

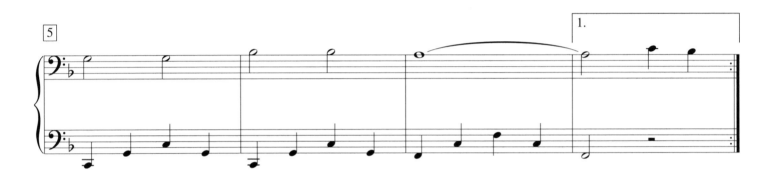

In My Own Little Corner

from CINEDRELLA

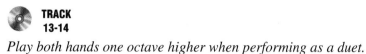

Lyrics by Oscar Hammerstein II
Music by Richard Rodgers
Arranged by Carolyn Miller

TRACK
13-14

Play both hands one octave higher when performing as a duet.

Dreamily, not too slow

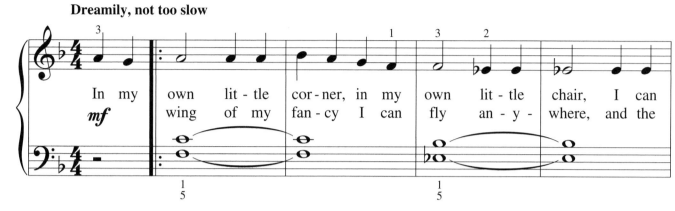

In my own lit-tle cor-ner, in my own lit-tle chair, I can
wing of my fan-cy I can fly an-y-where, and the

mf

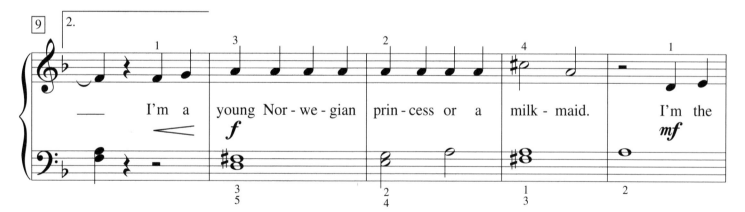

be what-ev-er I want to be. On the
world will o-pen its arms to me.

1.

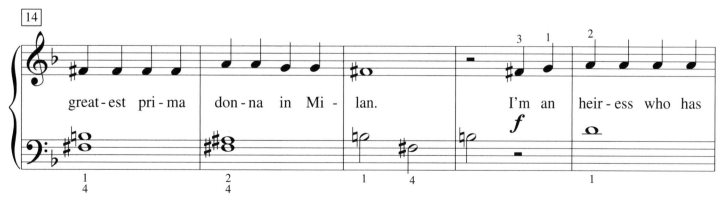

I'm a young Nor-we-gian prin-cess or a milk-maid. I'm the
f   *mf*

2.

great-est pri-ma don-na in Mi-lan. I'm an heir-ess who has
f

Accompaniment

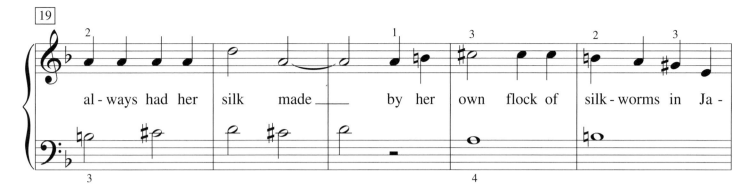

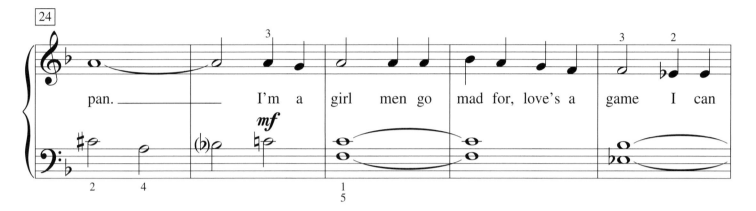

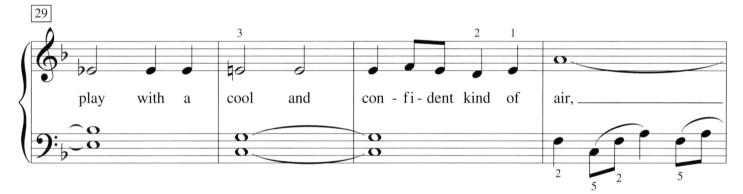

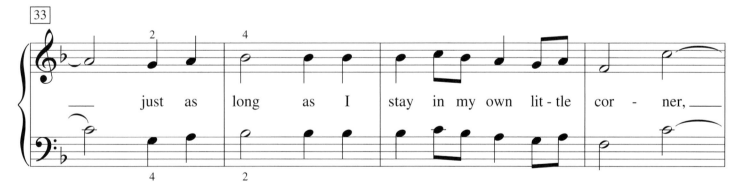

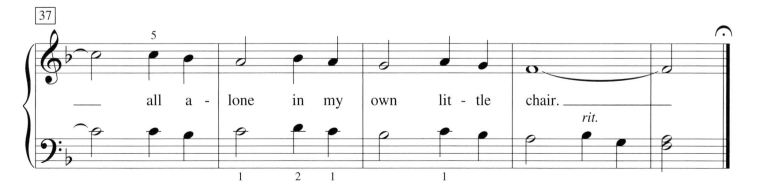

Sunrise, Sunset

from the Musical FIDDLER ON THE ROOF

Optional Teacher Accompaniment

Words by Sheldon Harnick
Music by Jerry Bock
Arranged by Carolyn Miller

Waltz tempo

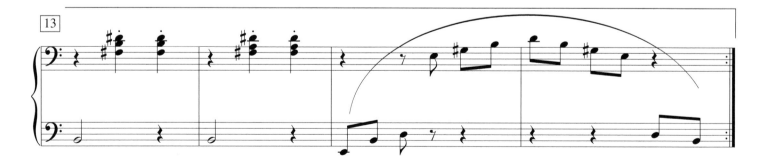

Sunrise, Sunset
from the Musical FIDDLER ON THE ROOF

Words by Sheldon Harnick
Music by Jerry Bock
Arranged by Carolyn Miller

TRACK 15-16

Play both hands one octave higher when performing as a duet.

Accompaniment

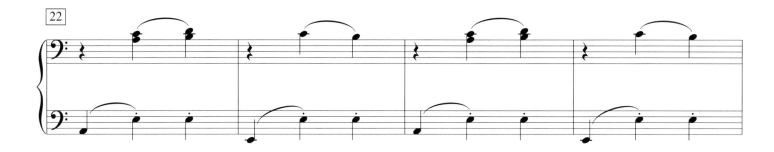

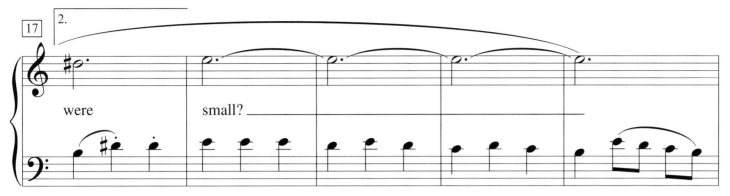

were   small? _____

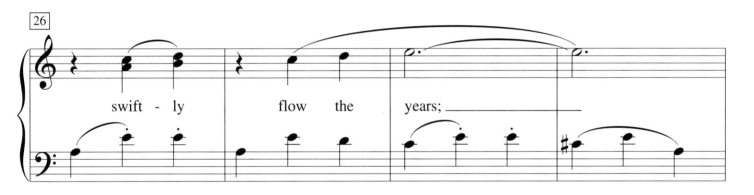

Sun - rise,   sun - set,   sun - rise,   sun - set,

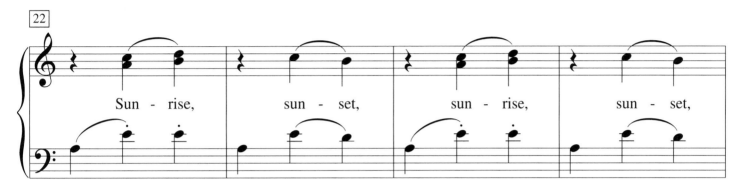

swift - ly   flow   the   years; _____

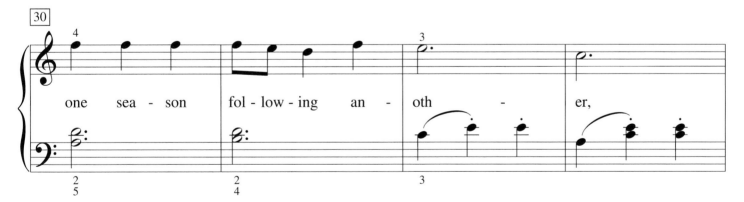

one   sea - son   fol - low - ing   an - oth -   er,

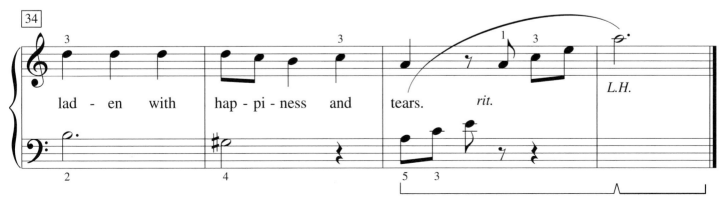

lad - en   with   hap - pi - ness   and   tears.   *rit.*

Gary, Indiana

from Meredith Willson's THE MUSIC MAN

Optional Teacher Accompaniment

By Meredith Willson
Arranged by Carolyn Miller

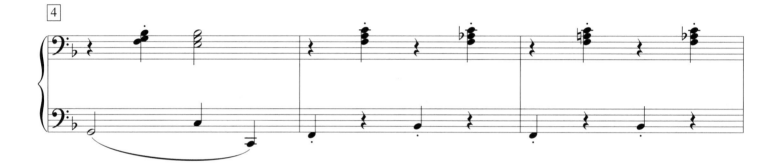

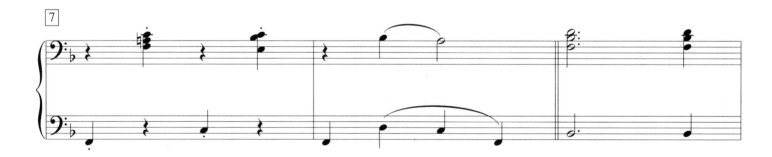

Gary, Indiana

from Meredith Willson's THE MUSIC MAN

TRACK
17-18

By Meredith Willson
Arranged by Carolyn Miller

Play both hands one octave higher when performing as a duet.

Accompaniment

say with-out a mo-ment of hes - i - ta - tion, there is just one place that can

light my face. Gar - y, In - di - an - a, Gar - y, In - di - an - a, not Lou - i - si -

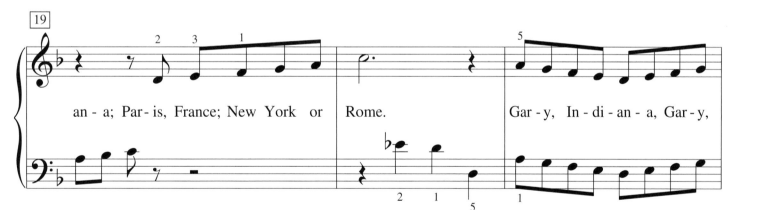

an - a; Par - is, France; New York or Rome. Gar - y, In - di - an - a, Gar - y,

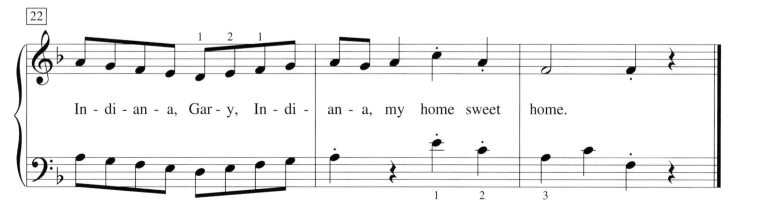

In - di - an - a, Gar - y, In - di - an - a, my home sweet home.

Climb Ev'ry Mountain

from THE SOUND OF MUSIC

Optional Teacher Accompaniment

Lyrics by Oscar Hammerstein II
Music by Richard Rodgers
Arranged by Carolyn Miller

Maestoso

Climb Ev'ry Mountain

from THE SOUND OF MUSIC

TRACK 19-20

Play both hands one octave higher when performing as a duet.

Lyrics by Oscar Hammerstein II
Music by Richard Rodgers
Arranged by Carolyn Miller

Maestoso

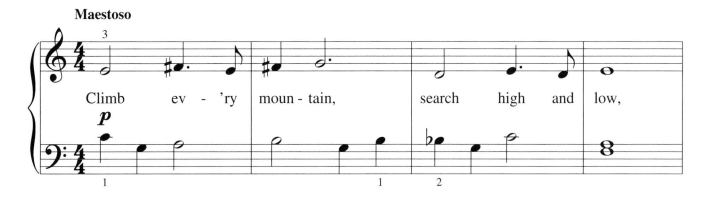

Climb ev - 'ry moun - tain, search high and low,

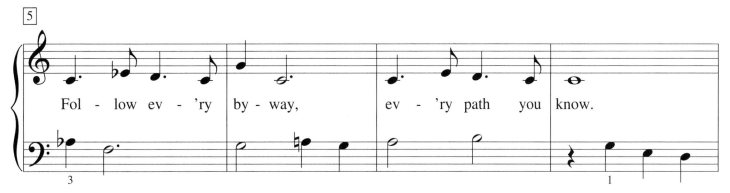

Fol - low ev - 'ry by - way, ev - 'ry path you know.

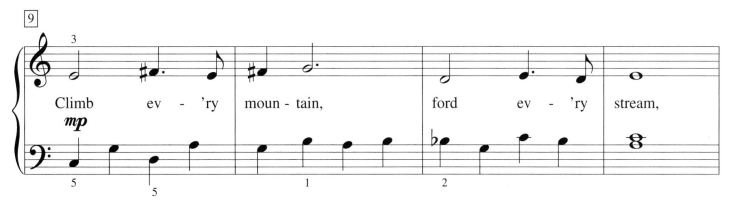

Climb ev - 'ry moun - tain, ford ev - 'ry stream,

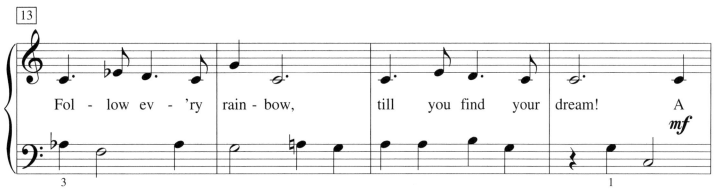

Fol - low ev - 'ry rain - bow, till you find your dream! A

Accompaniment

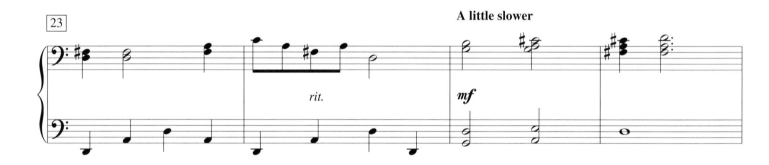

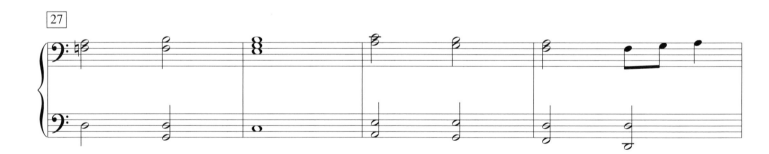

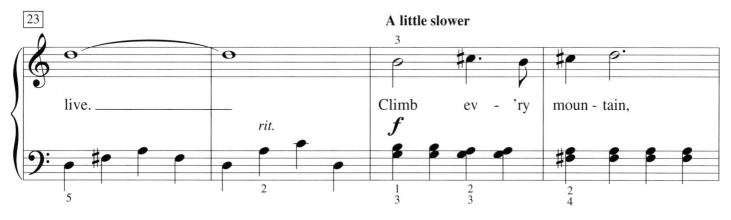

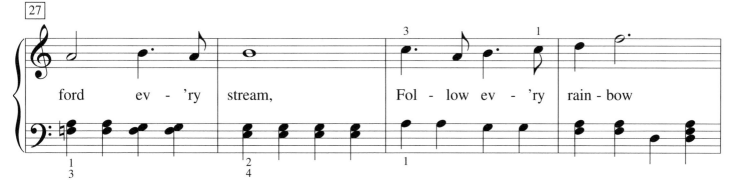

TEACHING LITTLE FINGERS
TO PLAY MORE

TEACHING LITTLE FINGERS TO PLAY MORE
by Leigh Kaplan
Teaching Little Fingers to Play More is a fun-filled and colorfully illustrated follow-up book to *Teaching Little Fingers to Play*. It strengthens skills learned while carefully easing the transition into John Thompson's *Modern Course, First Grade*.
00406137 Book only...$5.99
00406527 Book/CD $9.99

SUPPLEMENTARY SERIES
All books include optional teacher accompaniments.

CHILDREN'S SONGS
arr. Carolyn Miller
MID-ELEMENTARY LEVEL
10 songs: The Candy Man • Do-Re-Mi • I'm Popeye the Sailor Man • It's a Small World • Linus and Lucy • The Muppet Show Theme • Sesame Street Theme • Supercalifragilisticexpialidocious • Tomorrow.
00416810 Book only..$6.99
00416811 Book/CD $12.99

CLASSICS
arr. Randall Hartsell
MID-ELEMENTARY LEVEL
7 solos: Marche Slave • Over the Waves • Polovtsian Dance (from the opera *Prince Igor*) • Pomp and Circumstance • Rondeau • Waltz (from the ballet *Sleeping Beauty*) • William Tell Overture.
00406760 Book only..$5.99
00416513 Book/CD $10.99

DISNEY TUNES
arr. Glenda Austin
MID-ELEMENTARY LEVEL
9 songs, including: Circle of Life • Colors of the Wind • A Dream Is a Wish Your Heart Makes • A Spoonful of Sugar • Under the Sea • A Whole New World • and more.
00416750 Book only..$6.99
00416751 Book/CD $12.99

EASY DUETS
arr. Carolyn Miller
MID-ELEMENTARY LEVEL
9 equal-level duets: A Bicycle Built for Two • Blow the Man Down • Chopsticks • Do Your Ears Hang Low? • I've Been Working on the Railroad • The Man on the Flying Trapeze • Short'nin' Bread • Skip to My Lou • The Yellow Rose of Texas.
00416832 Book only..$5.99
00416833 Book/CD $10.99

JAZZ AND ROCK
Eric Baumgartner
MID-ELEMENTARY LEVEL
11 solos, including: Big Bass Boogie • Crescendo Rock • Funky Fingers • Jazz Waltz in G • Rockin' Rhythm • Squirrel Race • and more!
00406765 Book only..$5.99
00406828 Book/CD $10.99

JEWISH FAVORITES
arr. Eric Baumgartner
MID-ELEMENTARY LEVEL
7 songs: Ani Purim • Hava Nagila • Oyfn Pripetshik • Rozhinkes mit Mandlen • Russian Sher • Siman Tov • Zemer Atik.
00416755 Book only..$5.99
00416756 Book/CD $10.99

SONGS FROM MANY LANDS
arr. Carolyn C. Setliff
MID-ELEMENTARY LEVEL
7 solos: Ach, Du Lieber Augustin • The Ash Grove • Au Clair de la Lune • Mexican Hat Dance • My Bonnie • Tarantella • That's an Irish Lullaby.
00416688 Book only..$5.99
00416689 Book/CD $10.99

Also available:

AMERICAN TUNES
arr. Eric Baumgartner
MID-ELEMENTARY LEVEL
00406755 Book only..$5.99
00406820 Book/CD $10.99

BLUES AND BOOGIE
Carolyn Miller
MID-ELEMENTARY LEVEL
00406764 Book only..$5.99
00416512 Book/CD $10.99

CHRISTMAS CAROLS
arr. Carolyn Miller
MID-ELEMENTARY LEVEL
00406763 Book only..$5.99
00416475 Book/CD $10.99

CHRISTMAS CLASSICS
arr. Eric Baumgartner
MID-ELEMENTARY LEVEL
00416827 Book only..$6.99
00416826 Book/CD $12.99

CHRISTMAS FAVORITES
arr. Eric Baumgartner
MID-ELEMENTARY LEVEL
00416723 Book only..$6.99
00416724 Book/CD $12.99

FAMILIAR TUNES
arr. Glenda Austin
MID-ELEMENTARY LEVEL
00406761 Book only..$5.99
00416484 Book/CD $10.99

HYMNS
arr. Glenda Austin
MID-ELEMENTARY LEVEL
00406762 Book only..$5.99
00416485 Book/CD $10.99

RECITAL PIECES
Carolyn Miller
MID-ELEMENTARY LEVEL
00416540 Book only..$5.99
00416677 Book/CD $10.99

Complete song lists online at **www.halleonard.com**

EXCLUSIVELY DISTRIBUTED BY

WILLIS MUSIC

HAL•LEONARD®
CORPORATION
7777 W. BLUEMOUND RD. P.O. BOX 13819
MILWAUKEE, WISCONSIN 53213

Prices, contents, and availability subject to change without notice.